Table of Contents

3

Introduction

Delicious Recipes and Meal Plan to lose pounds, restore your Metabolism and healthy living

It's rare that a new diet trend gets a positive review from the health community, but for the most part, Noom has been praised for encouraging people to focus on healthier eating habits. A millennial-friendly app was created on which Noom is a diet service that actually doesn't re☐uire you to give up the foods that you love to eat.

Dieters, who pay a minimum of $59 each month for access to the app, are pushed to think about the Big Picture. Developed by a team of psychologists, the Noom diet is all about making long-term lifestyle shifts, unlike fad diets that might require a short-term fast or the shunning of certain food groups. It also connects dieters to live coaches and allows you to receive 1-on-1 health coaching during regular business hours.

Noom allows you to log exercise, weight loss over time and blood sugar levels as well as blood pressure. The diet itself begins after you take an in-depth quiz based on a series of lifestyle questions — calorie restrictions are recommended on a case by case basis, and they may recommend a diabetes management plan. Unlike the weight loss plan, the diabetes Noom plan is designed to particularly aid individuals suffering from both type 1 and type 2 diabetes, and may help prevent overweight or obese individuals from becoming pre-diabetic (it's even recognized by the Centers for Disease Control and Prevention).

If you're also trying to lose weight, there are endless programs and apps to choose from. And one that has over 45 million users is Noom. The diet plan has tons of solid reviews, but one part that can be confusing is the way Noom foods are grouped into lists or categories. Let's get into it.

Noom is an approach to dieting delivered via an app that combines food and calorie tracking with behavior change strategies. Like most diets, it helps consumers lose weight by creating a caloric deficit. Unlike most diets, there's an emphasis on the mental aspects of weight loss, and the app provides regular mindset strategies for helping consumers stay the course.

Sounds pretty good, huh? Well, you'll probably want to gauge whether the Noom diet method of food tracking makes sense for you and your lifestyle. This book contains everything you need to know about what to eat on the Noom diet, plus a comprehensive Noom foods list so you know exactly how to grocery shop and craft your meals.

What is the Noom diet—and how does the food logging work?

Noom claims to be the "last weight-loss program you'll ever need," according to its website. It's like having a trainer, nutritionist, and health coach all in one place: the Noom app. The app itself is free, but there are memberships that cost up to $59 a month.

Once you download it, the app asks for permission to access your smartphone's Health app, where it logs your exercise and you input everything you eat during the day (the app has a database of foods). Noom also uses a color-coding system to categorize foods. Noom uses a red, green, and yellow color system, instead of categorizing foods purely as 'good' or 'bad', to help the user gauge what is nutrient-dense and what is not.

What can you eat on Noom?

No foods are considered off-limits on the Noom diet. You simply group them using the color system, which broken down into the following:

Red signals the most calorically dense and/or least nutrient-dense foods, green are the least calorically dense and/or most nutrient-dense foods, and yellow foods fall somewhere in the middle. About 30 percent of your intake should come from green foods, 45 percent from yellow foods, and 25 percent from red foods.

With that in mind, here are some of the foods that fall under the each color category on Noom:

Green foods: Blueberries, apples, carrots, peppers, spinach, Brussels sprouts, broccoli, sweet potatoes, beets, berries, bananas, oats, whole-grain bread, quinoa, non-fat dairy products, egg whites

Yellow foods: Avocado, salmon, chicken, turkey, beans, tofu, whole eggs, tempeh, lean ground beef, black beans, chickpeas, low-fat dairy

Red foods: Olive oil and other oils, nuts and seeds, nut butters, dried fruit, beef, pork, full-fat dairy, bacon, French fries, burgers, potato chips, pizza, cake

It's worth noting that the app doesn't track macros. You're only shown what color the food falls under and its calorie content—no macronutrients (i.e., protein, carb, and fat content) or micronutrients (i.e., vitamins and minerals). For example, both olive oil and nut butter are categorized as 'red' foods, and while they're both fat-rich and calorically-dense, one also provides fiber and protein, the other does not.

Here's what a day of eating on the Noom diet might look like.

Here are two examples of what a day eating on Noom can look like and basic recipes.

Example one:

- **Breakfast**: Egg omelette with spinach, peppers, and mushrooms

- **Snack**: Fat-free Greek yogurt with blueberries or strawberries

- **Lunch**: Whole-grain wrap with hummus, grilled chicken, tomatoes, and cucumber

- **Dinner**: Seared salmon with baked Brussels sprouts and brown rice

- **Snack**: Oven roasted garlic chickpeas

Example two:

- **Breakfast**: Coffee with skim milk, ½ whole-wheat English muffin, 1 tbsp cream cheese, and a hard-boiled egg

- **Snack**: A small apple and 1 tbsp almond butter

- **Lunch**: Mixed green salad with tomato, cucumber, chicken breast, and 2 tbsp of vinaigrette dressing

- **Snack**: Baby carrots and ¼ cup hummus

- **Dinner**: 1 cup cooked ☐uinoa, ½ cup canned black beans, a bell pepper (sliced), 1/3 avocado, and ¼ cup salsa

- **Dessert**: Yasso mint chocolate chip frozen Greek yogurt bar

Recipes

Chicken & Spinach Soup with Fresh Pesto

This fragrant, Italian-flavored soup takes advantage of □uick-cooking ingredients-- boneless, skinless chicken breast, bagged baby spinach and canned beans. It features a simple homemade basil pesto swirled in at the end to add a fresh herb flavor. If you are very pressed for time, you can substitute 3 to 4 tablespoons of a store-bought basil pesto.

Total: 30 mins

Servings: 5

Ingredients

- 2 teaspoons 2 teaspoons plus 1 tablespoon extra-virgin olive oil, divided

- ½ cup carrot or diced red bell pepper

- 1 1 large boneless, skinless chicken breast (about 8 ounces), cut into ☐uarters

- 1 large 1 large clove garlic, minced

- 5 cups reduced-sodium chicken broth

- 1 ½ teaspoons dried marjoram

- 6 ounces 6 ounces baby spinach, coarsely chopped

- 1 (15 ounce) can 1 15-ounce can cannellini beans or great northern beans, rinsed

- ¼ cup grated Parmesan cheese

- ⅓ cup lightly packed fresh basil leaves

- 1 Freshly ground pepper to taste

- ¾ cup plain or herbed multigrain croutons for garnish (optional)

Directions

1. Heat 2 teaspoons oil in a large saucepan or Dutch oven over medium-high heat. Add carrot (or bell pepper) and chicken; cook, turning the chicken and stirring frequently, until the chicken begins to brown, 3 to 4 minutes. Add garlic and cook, stirring, for 1 minute more. Stir in broth and marjoram; bring to a boil over high heat. Reduce the heat and simmer, stirring occasionally, until the chicken is cooked through, about 5 minutes.

2. With a slotted spoon, transfer the chicken pieces to a clean cutting board to cool. Add spinach and beans to the pot and bring to a gentle boil. Cook for 5 minutes to blend the flavors.

3. Combine the remaining 1 tablespoon oil, Parmesan and basil in a food processor (a mini processor works well). Process until a coarse paste forms, adding a little water and scraping down the sides as necessary.

4. Cut the chicken into bite-size pieces. Stir the chicken and pesto into the pot. Season with pepper. Heat until hot. Garnish with croutons, if desired.

Nutrition Facts

Serving Size: About 1 1/2 Cups

Per Serving:

227 calories; protein 19.4g 39% DV; carbohydrates 18g 6% DV; dietary fiber 6g 24% DV; sugars 1.7g; fat 9.1g 14% DV; saturated fat 2g 10% DV; cholesterol 28.5mg 10% DV; vitamin a iu 3865.7IU 77% DV; vitamin c 29.4mg 49% DV; folate 76.7mcg 19% DV; calcium 92.8mg 9% DV; iron 2.1mg 12% DV; magnesium 43.7mg 16% DV; potassium 524.6mg 15% DV; sodium 211.4mg 9% DV; thiamin 0.1mg 6% DV.

Exchanges:

1 Starch, 1 Vegetable, 2 Lean Meat, 1 Fat

Creamy Garlic Pasta with Shrimp & Vegetables

Toss a garlicky, Middle Eastern-inspired yogurt sauce with pasta, shrimp, asparagus, peas and red bell pepper for a fresh, satisfying summer meal. Serve with: Slices of cucumber and tomato tossed with lemon juice and olive oil.

Total: 30 mins

Servings: 4

Ingredients

- 6 ounces whole-wheat spaghetti

- 12 ounces 12 ounces peeled and deveined raw shrimp (see Note), cut into 1-inch pieces

- 1 pound 1 bunch asparagus, trimmed and thinly sliced
- 1 large red bell pepper, thinly sliced
- 1 cup fresh or frozen peas
- 3 cloves garlic, chopped
- 1 ¼ teaspoons kosher salt
- 1 ½ cups nonfat or low-fat plain yogurt
- ¼ cup chopped flat-leaf parsley
- 3 tablespoons lemon juice
- 1 tablespoon extra-virgin olive oil
- ½ teaspoon freshly ground pepper
- ¼ cup 1/4 cup toasted pine nuts (see Tip; optional)

Directions

1. Bring a large pot of water to a boil. Add spaghetti and cook 2 minutes less than package directions. Add shrimp, asparagus, bell pepper and peas and cook until the pasta is tender and the shrimp are cooked, 2 to 4 minutes more. Drain well.

2. Mash garlic and salt in a large bowl until a paste forms. Whisk in yogurt, parsley, lemon juice, oil and pepper. Add the pasta mixture and toss to coat. Serve sprinkled with pine nuts (if using).

Tips

Both wild-caught and farm-raised shrimp can damage the surrounding ecosystems when not managed properly. Look for shrimp certified by an independent agency, such as Wild American Shrimp or Marine Stewardship Council. If you can't find certified shrimp, choose wild-caught shrimp from North America--it's more likely to be sustainably caught.

To toast pine nuts, place in a small dry skillet and cook over medium-low heat, stirring, until fragrant, 2 to 4 minutes.

Nutrition Facts

Serving Size: About 2 Cups

Per Serving:

361 calories; protein 28g 56% DV; carbohydrates 53.3g 17% DV; dietary fiber 10.2g 41% DV; sugars 13.6g; fat 5.6g 9% DV; saturated fat 1g 5% DV; cholesterol 109mg 36% DV; vitamin a iu 3525.6IU 71% DV; vitamin c 74.7mg 125% DV; folate 255.3mcg 64% DV; calcium 292.1mg 29% DV; iron 3.8mg 21% DV; magnesium 127.6mg 46% DV; potassium 826.8mg 23% DV; sodium 948.7mg 38% DV; thiamin 0.6mg 57% DV.

Exchanges:

2 1/2 Starch, 1 Vegetable, 1/2 Low-Fat Milk, 3 Lean Meat

Slow-Cooker Black Bean-Mushroom Chili

Black beans, earthy mushrooms and tangy tomatillos combine with a variety of spices and smoky chipotles to create a fantastic full-flavored chili. It can simmer in the slow cooker all day, which makes it perfect for a healthy supper when the end of your day is rushed.

Ingredients

- 1 pound 1 pound dried black beans, (2 1/2 cups), rinsed
- 1 tablespoon extra-virgin olive oil
- ¼ cup mustard seeds
- 2 tablespoons chili powder

- 1 ½ teaspoons 1 1/2 teaspoons cumin seeds, or ground cumin
- ½ teaspoon 1/2 teaspoon cardamom seeds, or ground cardamom
- 2 eaches medium onions, coarsely chopped
- 1 pound mushrooms, sliced
- 8 ounces 8 ounces tomatillos, (see Ingredient Note), husked, rinsed and coarsely chopped
- ¼ cup water
- 5 ½ cups 5 1/2 cups mushroom broth, or vegetable broth
- 1 ounce 1 6-ounce can tomato paste

- 2 tablespoons 1-2 tablespoons minced canned chipotle peppers in adobo sauce, (see Ingredient Note)
- 1 ¼ cups 1 1/4 cups grated Monterey Jack, or pepper Jack cheese
- ½ cup reduced-fat sour cream
- ½ cup chopped fresh cilantro
- 2 eaches limes, cut into wedges

Directions

1. Soak beans overnight in 2 ☐uarts water. (Alternatively, place beans and 2 quarts water in a large pot. Bring to a boil. Boil for 2 minutes. Remove from heat and let stand

for 1 hour.) Drain the beans, discarding soaking liquid.

2. Combine oil, mustard seeds, chili powder, cumin and cardamom in a 5- to 6-□uart Dutch oven. Place over high heat and stir until the spices sizzle, about 30 seconds. Add onions, mushrooms, tomatillos and water. Cover and cook, stirring occasionally, until the vegetables are juicy, 5 to 7 minutes. Uncover and stir often until the juices evaporate and the vegetables are lightly browned, 10 to 15 minutes. Add broth, tomato paste and chipotles; mix well.

3. Place the beans in a 5- to 6-quart slow cooker. Pour the hot vegetable mixture over the beans. Turn heat to high. Put the lid on and cook until the beans are creamy, 5 to 8 hours.

4. Garnish each serving with cheese, a dollop of sour cream and a sprinkling of cilantro. Serve with lime wedges.

5. Stovetop Variation:

6. Total: 4 1/2 hours

7. In Step 2, increase broth to 8 1/2 cups. Omit Step 3. Add the beans to the Dutch oven; cover and simmer the chili gently over low heat, stirring occasionally, until

the beans are creamy to bite, about 3
hours.

Tips

Make Ahead Tip: Cover and refrigerate for up
to 2 days or freeze for up to 3 months.

E☐uipment: 5- to 6-quart slow cooker

Ingredient notes: Chipotle peppers are dried,
smoked jalapeño peppers. Ground chipotle chile
pepper can be found in the specialty spice section
of most supermarkets. Chipotle chiles in adobo
sauce are smoked jalapeños packed in a flavorful
sauce. Look for the small cans with the Mexican
foods in large supermarkets. Once opened, they'll

31

keep up to 2 weeks in the refrigerator or 6 months in the freezer.

Tomatillos are tart, plum-size green fruits that look like small, husk-covered green tomatoes. Find them in the produce section near the tomatoes. Remove the outer husk and rinse them well before using.

For easy cleanup, try a slow-cooker liner. These heat-resistant, disposable liners fit neatly inside the insert and help prevent food from sticking to the bottom and sides of your slow cooker.

Nutrition Facts

Serving Size: 1 Cup

Per Serving:

299 calories; protein 18g 36% DV; carbohydrates 38.1g 12% DV; dietary fiber 12.8g 51% DV; sugars 4.6g; fat 9.6g 15% DV; saturated fat 3.9g 20% DV; cholesterol 19.7mg 7% DV; vitamin a iu 1029.7IU 21% DV; vitamin c 9mg 15% DV; folate 191.7mcg 48% DV; calcium 167.2mg 17% DV; iron 4.2mg 23% DV; magnesium 105.5mg 38% DV; potassium 721.6mg 20% DV; sodium 412.6mg 17% DV; thiamin 0.4mg 37% DV.

Exchanges:

2 Starch, 2 1/2 Vegetable, 1 Medium-Fat Protein, 1 Fat

Spaghetti S□uash with Roasted Tomatoes, Beans & Almond Pesto

Looking at a tangle of spaghetti squash tricks your brain into thinking you're about to eat a serving of eggy noodles, when in fact, you get a nice calorie and carb savings in this healthy recipe. Giving tomatoes a stint in a hot oven makes them candy-sweet.

Active: 45 mins

Total: 45 mins

Servings: 4

Ingredients

- 2 cups fresh basil leaves

- 1 cup fresh parsley leaves

- ½ cup grated Parmesan cheese

- ⅓ cup whole raw almonds

- 1 clove garlic

- 1 ½ tablespoons red-wine vinegar

- ¼ teaspoon kosher salt

- ¼ teaspoon ground pepper

- ¼ cup extra-virgin olive oil

- ¼ cup water

Spaghetti S□uash & Vegetables

- 1 3-pound spaghetti s□uash

- ¼ cup water

- 2 pints grape tomatoes, halved

- 1 tablespoon extra-virgin olive oil

- ¼ teaspoon kosher salt

- ¼ teaspoon ground pepper

- 1 cup canned cannellini beans, rinsed

Directions

1. To prepare pesto: Pulse basil, parsley, Parmesan, almonds, garlic, vinegar and 1/4 teaspoon each salt and pepper in a food processor until coarsely chopped, scraping down the sides. With the motor running, add 1/4 cup oil; process until well combined.

2. Add water to the pesto in the food processor; pulse to combine.

3. To prepare s☐uash & vegetables: Preheat oven to 400 degrees F. Line a rimmed baking sheet with foil.

4. Halve s☐uash lengthwise and scoop out the seeds. Place cut-side down in a microwave-safe dish and add water. Microwave on High until the flesh can be easily scraped with a fork, about 15 minutes.

5. Meanwhile, toss tomatoes with oil, salt and pepper in a large bowl. Transfer to the prepared baking sheet. Roast until soft and wrinkled, 10 to 12 minutes. Remove from the oven. Add beans and stir to combine.

6. Scrape the squash flesh into the bowl and divide among 4 plates. Top each portion with some of the tomato-bean mixture and about 3 tablespoons pesto sauce.

Tips

To make ahead: Refrigerate pesto (Step 1) for up to 5 days.

Tips: Turn leftovers into a pesto-turkey sandwich for lunch: Spread 1 1/2 Tbsp. leftover pesto on 2 slices toasted whole-wheat bread. Top with 3 oz. sliced deli turkey, 2 lettuce leaves and 2 tomato slices.

Nutrition Facts

Serving Size: 1 1/2 Cups Each

Per Serving:

400 calories; protein 12.2g 24% DV; carbohydrates 37.2g 12% DV; dietary fiber 10.4g 42% DV; sugars 11.8g; fat 26.4g 41% DV; saturated fat 4.4g 22% DV; cholesterol 7.8mg 3% DV; vitamin a iu 3779.5IU 76% DV; vitamin c 47.3mg 79% DV; folate 140.4mcg 35% DV; calcium 262mg 26% DV; iron 3.8mg 21% DV; magnesium 97.8mg 35% DV; potassium 1020.2mg 29% DV; sodium 498.5mg 20% DV.

Exchanges:

1 1/2 Starch, 1 Vegetable, 1/2 Lean Meat, 4 1/2 Fat

Creamy Mashed Cauliflower

This creamy cauliflower mash makes a perfect low-carb stand-in for mashed potatoes. Here we take simple mashed cauliflower and mix in garlic, buttermilk and a touch of butter to create a flavorful side dish that has about one-quarter of the calories of typical mashed potatoes. If you like, vary it by adding shredded low-fat cheese or chopped fresh herbs.

Total: 30 mins

Servings: 4

Ingredients

- 8 cups bite-size cauliflower florets (about 1 head)

- 4 cloves garlic, crushed and peeled

- ⅓ cup nonfat buttermilk (see Tip)

- 4 teaspoons extra-virgin olive oil, divided

- 1 teaspoon butter

- ½ teaspoon salt

- 1 Freshly ground pepper to taste

- 1 Snipped fresh chives for garnish

Directions

1. Place cauliflower florets and garlic in a steamer basket over boiling water, cover and steam until very tender, 12 to 15 minutes. (Alternatively, place florets and garlic in a microwave-safe bowl with 1/4

cup water, cover and microwave on High for 3 to 5 minutes.)

2. Place the cooked cauliflower and garlic in a food processor. Add buttermilk, 2 teaspoons oil, butter, salt and pepper; pulse several times, then process until smooth and creamy. Transfer to a serving bowl. Drizzle with the remaining 2 teaspoons oil and garnish with chives, if desired. Serve hot.

Tips

Tip: No buttermilk? You can use buttermilk powder prepared according to package directions.

Or make "sour milk": mix 1 tablespoon lemon juice or vinegar to 1 cup milk.

Nutrition Facts

Serving Size: 3/4 Cup

Per Serving:

107 calories; protein 4.5g 9% DV; carbohydrates 10.1g 3% DV; dietary fiber 4.3g 17% DV; sugars 4.8g; fat 6.5g 10% DV; saturated fat 1.4g 7% DV; cholesterol 2.9mg 1% DV; vitamin a iu 53.5IU 1% DV; vitamin c 86.9mg 145% DV; folate 85.5mcg 21% DV; calcium 41.2mg 4% DV; iron 0.7mg 4% DV; magnesium 18.4mg 7% DV; potassium 294mg 8% DV; sodium 338.8mg 14% DV; thiamin 0.1mg 9% DV.

Exchanges:

2 Vegetable, 1 1/2 Fat

Balsamic & Parmesan Roasted Cauliflower

Roasting isn't usually the first cooking method you think of for cauliflower but the results are quite delicious. The florets are cut into thick slices and tossed with extra-virgin olive oil and herbs. Wherever the flat surfaces come into contact with the hot roasting pan, a deep browning occurs that results in a sweet, nutty flavor.

Total: 35 mins

Servings: 4

Ingredients

- 8 cups 8 cups 1-inch-thick slices cauliflower florets, (about 1 large head; see Tip)
- 2 tablespoons extra-virgin olive oil
- 1 teaspoon dried marjoram
- ¼ teaspoon salt
- 1 Freshly ground pepper to taste
- 2 tablespoons balsamic vinegar
- ½ cup finely shredded Parmesan cheese

Directions

1. Preheat oven to 450 degrees F.
2. Toss cauliflower, oil, marjoram, salt and pepper in a large bowl. Spread on a large rimmed baking sheet and roast until

starting to soften and brown on the bottom, 15 to 20 minutes. Toss the cauliflower with vinegar and sprinkle with cheese. Return to the oven and roast until the cheese is melted and any moisture has evaporated, 5 to 10 minutes more.

Tips

Tip: To prepare florets from a whole head of cauliflower, remove outer leaves. Slice off the thick stem. With the head upside down and holding a knife at a 45° angle, slice into the smaller stems with a circular motion--removing a "plug" from the center of the head. Break or cut florets into the desired size.

Cut Down on Dishes: A rimmed baking sheet is great for everything from roasting to catching accidental drips and spills. For effortless cleanup and to keep your baking sheets in tip-top shape, line them with a layer of foil before each use.

Nutrition Facts

Serving Size: About 1 Cup

Per Serving:

152 calories; protein 6.8g 14% DV; carbohydrates 10.2g 3% DV; dietary fiber 3.2g 13% DV; sugars 5.1g; fat 10.2g 16% DV; saturated fat 2.9g 15% DV; cholesterol 7.2mg 2% DV; vitamin a iu 99IU 2% DV; vitamin c 75.2mg 125% DV; folate 90.1mcg 23% DV;

calcium 163mg 16% DV; iron 0.9mg 5% DV; magnesium 29.1mg 10% DV; potassium 519.2mg 15% DV; sodium 361.9mg 15% DV; thiamin 0.1mg 8% DV.

Exchanges:

1 Vegetable, 1/2 Lean Meat, 1 1/2 Fat

No-Peel Slow-Cooker Marinara Sauce

Store-bought pasta sauce just can't compare to homemade marinara--and the slow cooker makes marinara from scratch much easier. This fresh tomato recipe was developed to preserve the summer bounty from your garden or farmers' market; it freezes well for up to 6 months so you can pull out pasta or pizza sauce anytime.

Keeping the skins on makes it even easier, plus they contain pectin, which helps thicken the sauce.

Active: 25 mins

Total: 10 hrs 30 mins

Servings: 18

Ingredients

- 6 pounds tomatoes

- 2 cups chopped onion

- ¼ cup extra-virgin olive oil

- 1 (6 ounce) can tomato paste

- 3 tablespoons finely chopped garlic

- 2 tablespoons finely chopped fresh oregano

- 2 tablespoons balsamic vinegar

- 4 teaspoons granulated sugar

- 1 ½ teaspoons salt, divided

- 1 teaspoon Ground pepper or crushed red pepper to taste

Directions

1. Cut tomatoes in half crosswise. Gently s☐ueeze out the seeds and discard (don't worry if you don't get them all). Mix onion, oil, tomato paste, garlic, oregano, vinegar, sugar and 1 teaspoon salt in a 6-quart or larger slow cooker. Place the tomatoes on top.

2. Cover and cook for 2 hours on High or 4 hours on Low.

3. Puree with an immersion blender or in a regular blender in batches until chunky. (Use caution when pureeing hot li□uids.) Placing the lid askew, cook until thickened, about 3 hours more on High or 6 hours more on Low.

4. Season with the remaining 1/2 teaspoon salt and pepper (or crushed red pepper) to taste. Puree further, if desired. Serve hot or let cool completely before refrigerating for up to 5 days or freezing for up to 6 months.

Tips

To make ahead: Refrigerate for up to 5 days or freeze for up to 6 months.

Equipment: 6-qt. or larger slow cooker

Nutrition Facts

Serving Size: 1/2 Cup

Per Serving:

82 calories; protein 1.7g 3% DV; carbohydrates 10.3g 3% DV; dietary fiber 2.5g 10% DV; sugars 6.7g; fat 3.7g 6% DV; saturated fat 0.5g 2% DV; cholesterolmg; vitamin a iu 1241IU 25% DV; vitamin c 21.1mg 35% DV; folate 24mcg 6% DV; calcium 20.5mg 2% DV; iron 0.7mg 4% DV; magnesium 17.5mg 6% DV; potassium 447.9mg

13% DV; sodium 231.9mg 9% DV; added sugar 0.9g.

Slow-Roasted Tomatoes

Slowly cooking summer-ripe tomatoes in a low oven makes them candy-sweet. Turn to this recipe to preserve the summer bounty from your garden or farmers' market; it freezes well for up to 6 months. Tuck these tasty bites into sandwiches; stir them into risotto; or chop them and mix with Kalamata olives, olive oil and fresh herbs to scoop up with pita chips.

Active: 30 mins

Total: 5 hrs 30 mins

Servings: 14

Ingredients

- 8 pounds plum tomatoes or 8 pints cherry tomatoes
- ¼ cup extra-virgin olive oil
- ⅔ cup thinly sliced garlic
- ¼ cup chopped fresh herbs, such as oregano, basil, thyme and/or parsley
- ½ teaspoon salt
- ½ teaspoon ground pepper

Directions

1. Position oven racks in upper and lower thirds of oven; preheat to 300 degrees F. Line 2 rimmed baking sheets with parchment paper or silicone baking mats.

2. Halve tomatoes (□uarter any large plum tomatoes). Divide the tomatoes between the prepared baking sheets, placing them cut-side up. Drizzle with oil and sprinkle with garlic, herbs, salt and pepper. Bake the tomatoes, switching the pans from top to bottom and back to front halfway through, until shriveled, about 2 1/2 hours for cherry tomatoes and about 5 hours for plum tomatoes. Serve warm or at room temperature. Let cool completely before refrigerating for up to 1 week or freezing for up to 6 months.

Tips

To make ahead: Refrigerate for up to 1 week or freeze for up to 6 months.

Nutrition Facts

Serving Size: ½ Cup

Per Serving:

89 calories; protein 2.5g 5% DV; carbohydrates 11.5g 4% DV; dietary fiber 3g 12% DV; sugars 6.3g; fat 4.5g 7% DV; saturated fat 0.6g 3% DV; cholesterolmg; vitamin a iu 2027IU 41% DV; vitamin c 35.6mg 59% DV; folate 36.6mcg 9% DV; calcium 37.8mg 4% DV; iron 0.9mg 5% DV; magnesium 28.5mg 10% DV; potassium 591.1mg 17% DV; sodium 96.3mg 4% DV.

No-Peel Slow-Cooker Marinara Sauce

Store-bought pasta sauce just can't compare to homemade marinara--and the slow cooker makes marinara from scratch much easier. This fresh tomato recipe was developed to preserve the summer bounty from your garden or farmers' market; it freezes well for up to 6 months so you can pull out pasta or pizza sauce anytime. Keeping the skins on makes it even easier, plus they contain pectin, which helps thicken the sauce.

Active: 25 mins

Total: 10 hrs 30 mins

Servings: 18

Ingredients

- 6 pounds tomatoes

- 2 cups chopped onion

- ¼ cup extra-virgin olive oil

- 1 (6 ounce) can tomato paste

- 3 tablespoons finely chopped garlic

- 2 tablespoons finely chopped fresh oregano

- 2 tablespoons balsamic vinegar

- 4 teaspoons granulated sugar

- 1 ½ teaspoons salt, divided

- 1 teaspoon Ground pepper or crushed red pepper to taste

Directions

1. Cut tomatoes in half crosswise. Gently squeeze out the seeds and discard (don't worry if you don't get them all). Mix onion, oil, tomato paste, garlic, oregano, vinegar, sugar and 1 teaspoon salt in a 6-□uart or larger slow cooker. Place the tomatoes on top.

2. Cover and cook for 2 hours on High or 4 hours on Low.

3. Puree with an immersion blender or in a regular blender in batches until chunky. (Use caution when pureeing hot liquids.) Placing the lid askew, cook until thickened, about 3 hours more on High or 6 hours more on Low.

59

4. Season with the remaining 1/2 teaspoon salt and pepper (or crushed red pepper) to taste. Puree further, if desired. Serve hot or let cool completely before refrigerating for up to 5 days or freezing for up to 6 months.

Tips

To make ahead: Refrigerate for up to 5 days or freeze for up to 6 months.

E□uipment: 6-□t. or larger slow cooker

Nutrition Facts

Serving Size: ½ Cup

Per Serving:

82 calories; protein 1.7g 3% DV; carbohydrates 10.3g 3% DV; dietary fiber 2.5g 10% DV; sugars 6.7g; fat 3.7g 6% DV; saturated fat 0.5g 2% DV; cholesterolmg; vitamin a iu 1241IU 25% DV; vitamin c 21.1mg 35% DV; folate 24mcg 6% DV; calcium 20.5mg 2% DV; iron 0.7mg 4% DV; magnesium 17.5mg 6% DV; potassium 447.9mg 13% DV; sodium 231.9mg 9% DV; added sugar 0.9g.

Slow-Roasted Tomatoes

Slowly cooking summer-ripe tomatoes in a low oven makes them candy-sweet. Turn to this recipe to preserve the summer bounty from your garden or farmers' market; it freezes well for up to 6 months. Tuck these tasty bites into sandwiches; stir them into risotto; or chop them and mix with Kalamata olives, olive oil and fresh herbs to scoop up with pita chips.

Active: 30 mins

Total: 5 hrs 30 mins

Servings: 14

Ingredients

- 8 pounds plum tomatoes or 8 pints cherry tomatoes
- ¼ cup extra-virgin olive oil
- ⅔ cup thinly sliced garlic
- ¼ cup chopped fresh herbs, such as oregano, basil, thyme and/or parsley
- ½ teaspoon salt

- ½ teaspoon ground pepper

Directions

1. Position oven racks in upper and lower thirds of oven; preheat to 300 degrees F. Line 2 rimmed baking sheets with parchment paper or silicone baking mats.

2. Halve tomatoes (quarter any large plum tomatoes). Divide the tomatoes between the prepared baking sheets, placing them cut-side up. Drizzle with oil and sprinkle with garlic, herbs, salt and pepper. Bake the tomatoes, switching the pans from top to bottom and back to front halfway through, until shriveled, about 2 1/2 hours

for cherry tomatoes and about 5 hours for plum tomatoes. Serve warm or at room temperature. Let cool completely before refrigerating for up to 1 week or freezing for up to 6 months.

Tips

To make ahead: Refrigerate for up to 1 week or freeze for up to 6 months.

Nutrition Facts

Serving Size: ½ Cup

Per Serving:

89 calories; protein 2.5g 5% DV; carbohydrates 11.5g 4% DV; dietary fiber 3g 12% DV; sugars

6.3g; fat 4.5g 7% DV; saturated fat 0.6g 3% DV; cholesterolmg; vitamin a iu 2027IU 41% DV; vitamin c 35.6mg 59% DV; folate 36.6mcg 9% DV; calcium 37.8mg 4% DV; iron 0.9mg 5% DV; magnesium 28.5mg 10% DV; potassium 591.1mg 17% DV; sodium 96.3mg 4% DV.

Mango Raspberry Smoothie

A s☐ueeze of lemon juice adds bright flavor to this frozen fruit smoothie. Mango provides plenty of sweetness without having to add juice, but if it's too tart for you, a touch of agave will do the trick.

Active: 5 mins

Total: 5 mins

Servings: 1

Ingredients

- ½ cup water

- ¼ medium avocado

- 1 tablespoon lemon juice

- ¾ cup frozen mango

- ¼ cup frozen raspberries

- 1 tablespoon agave (Optional)

Directions

1. Add water, avocado, lemon juice, mango, raspberries and agave (if using) to a blender. Blend until smooth.

Nutrition Facts

Serving Size: 1 ½ Cups

Per Serving:

188 calories; protein 1.5g 3% DV; carbohydrates 32.3g 10% DV; dietary fiber 6.2g 25% DV; sugars 23.3g; fat 7.4g 11% DV; saturated fat 1.1g 5% DV; cholesterolmg; vitamin a iu 1102IU 22% DV; vitamin c 51.6mg 86% DV; folate 43.8mcg 11% DV; calcium 34.5mg 3% DV; iron 0.9mg 5% DV; magnesium 16.7mg 6% DV; potassium 260.6mg 7% DV; sodium 7.7mg.

Shaved Summer S☐uash Salad with Ricotta Salata & Charred Fennel

While spinach is a good leafy substitute for the sorrel in this salad, sometimes use thinly sliced raw rhubarb to mimic sorrel's tangy flavor in this summer squash salad.

Active: 30 mins

Total: 30 mins

Servings: 6

Ingredients

- 1 ¾ pounds small zucchini and/or summer s☐uash, trimmed
- 3 tablespoons extra-virgin olive oil, divided
- 4 eaches baby fennel bulbs or 1 large fennel bulb, fronds reserved for garnish
- 1 cup baby sorrel (see Tip) or spinach

- ½ cup fresh opal basil leaves, chopped

- ½ cup flat-leaf parsley leaves, chopped

- ¼ cup coarsely chopped fresh chives

- 1 1 to 2 tablespoons lemon juice

- 2 ounces shaved ricotta salata cheese

- ½ teaspoon flaky sea salt

- ½ teaspoon ground pepper

Directions

1. Preheat grill to medium-high

2. Using a mandoline or vegetable peeler, thinly slice s□uash lengthwise until you encounter the seeds. Discard the seedy centers. Place the s□uash ribbons in a large bowl and toss with 1 tablespoon oil.

3. If using a large fennel bulb, cut in half lengthwise; leave baby fennel whole. Oil the grill rack. Grill the fennel, flipping occasionally, until tender and slightly charred, 10 to 12 minutes. Transfer to a rimmed baking sheet and drizzle with 1 tablespoon oil. When cool enough to handle, cut crosswise into 3/4-inch-wide pieces.

4. Add the fennel to the s□uash along with sorrel (or spinach), basil, parsley, chives and lemon juice to taste; toss. Sprinkle the salad with ricotta salata, salt, pepper and fennel fronds, if using. Drizzle with the remaining 1 tablespoon oil.

70

Tips

Nutrition bonus: Vitamin C (83% daily value), Vitamin A (48% dv).

Tip: Sorrel, a lemony-tasting, leafy green herb, contains high amounts of oxalic acid, which imparts a tart flavor. Spinach--along with a good s□ueeze of lemon juice--makes an excellent substitute.

Nutrition Facts

Serving Size: 1 1/3 Cups

Per Serving:

147 calories; protein 5.1g 10% DV; carbohydrates 9.9g 3% DV; dietary fiber 4g 16%

DV; sugars 5.3g; fat 10.1g 16% DV; saturated fat 3.1g 16% DV; cholesterol 2.4mg 1% DV; vitamin a iu 2393IU 48% DV; vitamin c 50mg 83% DV; folate 65.4mcg 16% DV; calcium 74.1mg 7% DV; iron 1.9mg 11% DV; magnesium 61.8mg 22% DV; potassium 716.3mg 20% DV; sodium 249.8mg 10% DV.

Cherry Smoothie

The combination of oat milk, vanilla extract and sweet cherries makes this recipe taste like a cherry pie smoothie. Adding a bit of brown sugar boosts that nostalgia even more.

Active: 5 mins

Total: 5 mins

Servings: 1

Ingredients

- ½ cup oat milk

- 1 tablespoon almond butter

- 1 teaspoon cocoa powder

- ½ teaspoon vanilla extract

- 1 cup frozen dark sweet cherries

- 1 tablespoon brown sugar (Optional)

Directions

1. Add oat milk, almond butter, cocoa, vanilla, cherries and sugar (if using) to a blender. Blend until smooth.

Nutrition Facts

Serving Size: 1 ½ Cups

Per Serving:

232 calories; protein 5.7g 11% DV; carbohydrates 31.5g 10% DV; dietary fiber 5.8g 23% DV; sugars 21g; fat 9.1g 14% DV; saturated fat 1.2g 6% DV; cholesterolmg; vitamin a iu 100.2IU 2% DV; vitamin c 9mg 15% DV; folate 9.1mcg 2% DV; calcium 307.8mg 31% DV; iron 1.5mg 8% DV; magnesium 53.6mg 19% DV; potassium 242mg 7% DV; sodium 86.7mg 4% DV; added sugar 2g.

Chicken Hummus Bowls

The spiced chicken atop these bowls is ready fast with the help of the broiler. Serve with warm whole-wheat pita for scooping up extra hummus at the bottom of the bowl.

Active: 25 mins

Total: 25 mins

Servings: 4

Ingredients

- 1 pound boneless, skinless chicken thighs, trimmed and cut into 1-inch pieces
- 3 tablespoons extra-virgin olive oil, divided
- 1 teaspoon ground cumin
- 1 teaspoon paprika

- ¼ teaspoon cayenne pepper

- ¼ teaspoon salt, divided

- 2 cloves garlic, finely chopped

- 2 tablespoons lemon juice

- 2 cups hummus

- 1 English cucumber, halved lengthwise and sliced

- 1 pint cherry tomatoes, halved

- ¼ cup slivered red onion

- ¼ cup chopped fresh parsley

Directions

1. Position rack in upper third of oven; preheat broiler to high. Line a rimmed baking sheet with foil.

2. Toss chicken with 1 tablespoon oil, cumin, paprika, cayenne and 1/8 teaspoon salt. Spread evenly on the prepared pan. Broil until just cooked through, 5 to 7 minutes.

3. Meanwhile, mash garlic and the remaining 1/8 teaspoon salt into a paste with a fork. Transfer to a medium bowl and whisk in lemon juice and the remaining 2 tablespoons oil. Add the chicken and let stand for 5 minutes, stirring occasionally.

4. Divide hummus among 4 shallow bowls or plates. Top with the chicken and any remaining dressing, cucumber, tomatoes, onion and parsley.

Nutrition Facts

Serving Size: ½ Cup Each Hummus, Chicken, Tomatoes & Cucumber

Per Serving:

485 calories; protein 31.1g 62% DV; carbohydrates 27.3g 9% DV; dietary fiber 9.6g 38% DV; sugars 4.4g; fat 29.4g 45% DV; saturated fat 5.2g 26% DV; cholesterol 104.1mg 35% DV; vitamin a iu 1364IU 27% DV; vitamin c 22.5mg 38% DV; folate 135.5mcg 34% DV; calcium 94.7mg 10% DV; iron 4.9mg 27% DV; magnesium 134.1mg 48% DV; potassium 886.2mg 25% DV; sodium 712.1mg 29% DV.

Stuffed Eggplant with Couscous & Almonds

Smoky almonds, meaty eggplant and whole-grain couscous with herbs make this meal plenty satisfying. Harissa gives the creamy sauce a little kick.

Active: 30 mins

Total: 30 mins

Servings: 4

Ingredients

- ⅔ cup water plus 1 tablespoon, divided

- ½ cup whole-wheat couscous (see Tip)

- ½ teaspoon salt, divided

- 2 medium eggplants (about 1 pound each)

- 3 tablespoons extra-virgin olive oil, divided

- ¼ teaspoon ground pepper

- 1 clove garlic, finely chopped

- ⅓ cup mayonnaise

- 2 eaches teaspoons harissa paste or ½ teaspoon harissa seasoning

- ½ cup chopped smoke-flavored almonds

- ½ cup chopped fresh parsley

Directions

1. Preheat grill to medium-high.

2. Combine 2/3 cup water, couscous and 1/8 teaspoon salt in a small saucepan. Bring to

a boil over high heat. Remove from heat, cover and set aside.

3. Halve eggplants through the stem; brush the cut sides with 2 tablespoons oil and sprinkle with ¼ teaspoon salt and pepper. Grill the eggplants, flipping once halfway, until charred and tender, 10 to 12 minutes. Let cool for 5 minutes.

4. Meanwhile, mash garlic with the remaining 1/8 teaspoon salt on a cutting board with a fork. Combine the garlic paste, mayonnaise, harissa and the remaining 1 tablespoon water in a small bowl.

5. Leaving a ¼ -inch-thick wall, carefully scoop out the eggplant flesh and chop. Stir

the eggplant flesh into the couscous along with almonds, parsley and the remaining 1 tablespoon oil. Mound the filling in the eggplant shells. Serve with the sauce.

Tips

Tip: Light and fluffy couscous is made by rolling coarse semolina flour, resulting in small round granules. Choosing a whole-wheat variety gives you three times the fiber of white.

Nutrition Facts

Serving Size: ½ Eggplant & 2 Tbsp. Sauce

Per Serving:

457 calories; protein 9.2g 18% DV; carbohydrates 35.4g 11% DV; dietary fiber 10.9g 44% DV; sugars 8.6g; fat 33g 51% DV; saturated fat 4.2g 21% DV; cholesterol 7.7mg 3% DV; vitamin a iu 696.8IU 14% DV; vitamin c 15.4mg 26% DV; folate 62.3mcg 16% DV; calcium 85.7mg 9% DV; iron 2.3mg 13% DV; magnesium 36.6mg 13% DV; potassium 570mg 16% DV; sodium 521.9mg 21% DV.

Summer Vegetable Gnocchi Salad

This riff on pasta salad is best served warm while the gnocchi are nice and tender. Plus, the grilled veggies taste extra-good fresh off the fire in this easy gnocchi recipe.

Active: 40 mins

Total: 40 mins

Servings: 4

Ingredients

- 1 (16 ounce) package whole-wheat gnocchi

- 1 small eggplant, sliced lengthwise into ½-inch planks

- 1 medium zucchini, sliced lengthwise into ½-inch planks

- 1 medium yellow squash, sliced lengthwise into ½-inch planks

- 1 ear corn, husked

- ½ medium red onion, cut into ½-inch-thick rings

- 4 tablespoons extra-virgin olive oil, divided

- 2 tablespoons balsamic vinegar

- 2 tablespoons chopped fresh basil

- 2 cloves garlic, grated

- ½ teaspoon ground pepper

- ¼ teaspoon salt

- ½ cup crumbled feta cheese

Directions

1. Preheat grill to medium-high.

2. Boil gnocchi according to package directions. Drain.

3. Meanwhile, brush eggplant, zucchini, s□uash, corn and onion with 2 tablespoons oil. Grill the vegetables, turning

occasionally, until charred and tender, 6 to 10 minutes total. Transfer to a cutting board. Remove the corn kernels from the cob and cut the other vegetables into bite-size pieces.

4. Whisk the remaining 2 tablespoons oil, vinegar, basil, garlic, pepper and salt in a large bowl. Add the gnocchi and the vegetables and toss to coat. Serve sprinkled with feta.

Nutrition Facts

Serving Size: 2 Cups

Per Serving:

445 calories; protein 13g 26% DV; carbohydrates 60.1g 19% DV; dietary fiber 9.1g 36% DV; sugars 12.1g; fat 19g 29% DV; saturated fat 4.4g 22% DV; cholesterol 12.6mg 4% DV; vitamin a iu 527.5IU 11% DV; vitamin c 31.7mg 53% DV; folate 85.3mcg 21% DV; calcium 128.4mg 13% DV; iron 2.4mg 13% DV; magnesium 61.8mg 22% DV; potassium 921.1mg 26% DV; sodium 691.2mg 28% DV.

Japanese Shiitake & Vegetable Rice (Takikomi Gohan)

Dashi gives this vegetable rice recipe its savory depth. Rinsing the rice may seem like an extraneous step but it removes some of the surface starch for fluffier rice. And soaking the rice in seasoned dashi before cooking infuses the dish with more flavor.

Active: 20 mins

Total: 2 hrs 30 mins

Servings: 6

Ingredients

- 1 ½ cups short-grain brown rice

- 2 ½ cups Dashi Stock (see Associated Recipes)

- 2 tablespoons mirin

- 2 tablespoons reduced-sodium tamari

- 1 pinch Pinch of salt

- 6 ounces shiitake mushrooms, sliced 1/4 inch thick

- ½ cup diced carrot

- 2 eaches scallions, thinly sliced on the diagonal, whites and greens separated

- ¼ cup frozen peas

Directions

1. Put rice in a large saucepan and add water to cover by 1 inch. Swish with your fingers to loosen the surface starch. Pour off the water and repeat two or three times, or until the water is nearly clear. Pour the rice into a fine-mesh sieve and let drain for 5 minutes. Shake the sieve a few times, then return the rice to the pan.

2. Add dashi, mirin, tamari and salt. Let stand for 30 minutes.

3. Bring the mixture to a lively simmer over medium-high heat, stirring occasionally. Reduce heat to maintain a low simmer, cover and cook for 30 minutes. Place mushrooms, carrot and scallion whites on top, cover and cook until the rice and vegetables are tender, about 15 minutes more.

4. Remove from heat and let stand for 10 minutes. Scatter peas over the top, then fluff the rice and combine with the peas. Cover and let stand until the peas are

thawed, about 10 minutes. Stir in scallion greens before serving.

Nutrition Facts

Serving Size: 1 Cup

Per Serving:

188 calories; protein 4.8g 10% DV; carbohydrates 41.3g 13% DV; dietary fiber 4.5g 18% DV; sugars 3.1g; fat 1.7g 3% DV; saturated fatg; cholesterolmg; vitamin a iu 1946.7IU 39% DV; vitamin c 2.6mg 4% DV; folate 11.9mcg 3% DV; calcium 15.7mg 2% DV; iron 1.3mg 7% DV; magnesium 14.1mg 5% DV; potassium 169mg 5% DV; sodium 291.2mg 12% DV.

Chopped Salad with Cornbread Croutons

Active: 25 mins

Total: 25 mins

Servings: 6

Ingredients

- ½ cup cubed cornbread

- 6 cups chopped romaine lettuce

- 1 ½ cups thinly sliced red cabbage

- ½ cup canned black-eyed peas, rinsed

- ½ cup frozen roasted corn kernels, thawed

- ½ cup halved cherry tomatoes

- ¼ cup diced pimientos, rinsed

- ½ cup prepared ranch dressing

- ½ cup thinly sliced red onion

Directions

1. Preheat oven to 350 degrees F.

2. Spread cornbread cubes in a small baking pan. Bake, stirring once halfway, until golden, 8 to 10 minutes. Let cool.

3. Combine lettuce, cabbage, black-eyed peas, corn, tomatoes and pimientos in a large bowl. Add dressing and toss to coat. Serve topped with onion and the cornbread croutons.

Tips

Nutrition Bonus: Vitamin A (92% daily value), Vitamin C (35% daily value), Folate (22% daily value), Added Sugars: 0g

Nutrition Facts

Serving Size: 1 1/3 Cups

Per Serving:

160 calories; protein 3.2g 6% DV; carbohydrates 14.7g 5% DV; dietary fiber 3.3g 13% DV; sugars 5.1g; fat 10.2g 16% DV; saturated fat 1.7g 9% DV; cholesterol 9.2mg 3% DV; vitamin a iu 4609IU 92% DV; vitamin c 21mg 35% DV; folate 88.3mcg 22% DV; calcium 46.4mg 5% DV; iron 1.1mg 6% DV; magnesium 19.9mg 7% DV; potassium 269.9mg 8% DV; sodium 272mg 11% DV.

Baked Fish & Kale Lavash Wraps

Controlling moisture is key to avoiding soggy lavash in this recipe, so be sure to s☐ueeze as much liquid from the greens as possible. Look for lavash with large sandwich wraps at the grocery store. We prefer the flakier texture of rectangular lavash--the round ones are more like big flour tortillas and bake up a little gummy.

Active: 25 mins

Total: 45 mins

Servings: 4

Ingredients

- 5 ounces baby kale or baby spinach

- 3 tablespoons coarsely chopped fresh tarragon and/or dill
- 2 tablespoons finely chopped scallions
- ½ teaspoon kosher salt, divided
- ⅛ teaspoon plus 1/4 teaspoon ground pepper, divided
- 1 pound cod, halibut or barramundi, skinned and cut into 4 portions
- 4 sheets lavash
- 6 teaspoons extra-virgin olive oil, divided
- ¼ cup Very Versatile Roasted Red Pepper Sauce, plus more for serving

Directions

1. Preheat oven to 375 degrees F. Line a baking sheet with parchment paper and coat with cooking spray. Put a kettle of water on to boil.

2. Put greens in a bowl. Cover with boiling water and let wilt for about 5 minutes. Drain and squeeze out excess moisture. Chop and return to the bowl. Mix in tarragon (and/or dill), scallions, 1/4 teaspoon salt and 1/8 teaspoon pepper.

3. Pat fish dry and season with the remaining 1/4 teaspoon each salt and pepper.

4. To make each wrap, place a lavash sheet on your work surface with a short side closest to you. Brush with 1 teaspoon oil

and place a portion of fish about 2 inches from the bottom edge. Smear 1 tablespoon red pepper sauce on the fish and top with one-fourth of the greens. Roll up like a burrito and place seam-side down on the prepared pan. Brush the wraps with the remaining 2 teaspoons oil.

5. Bake until the lavash is browned and crisp, rotating the pan from back to front halfway through, 20 to 30 minutes. Serve immediately with additional sauce, if desired.

Nutrition Facts

Serving Size: 1 Wrap

Per Serving:

392 calories; protein 24.3g 49% DV; carbohydrates 45.7g 15% DV; dietary fiber 10g 40% DV; sugars 3.4g; fat 9.5g 15% DV; saturated fat 1.5g 8% DV; cholesterol 44.6mg 15% DV; vitamin a iu 2486.8IU 50% DV; vitamin c 45.7mg 76% DV; folate 21.5mcg 5% DV; calcium 154.5mg 16% DV; iron 0.9mg 5% DV; magnesium 23.8mg 9% DV; potassium 520.4mg 15% DV; sodium 844mg 34% DV.

Sichuan Fava Bean, Pea Sprout & Radish Salad

This fresh and spicy salad features fava beans, which besides adding heft to this radish salad are a main ingredient in the iconic chili bean paste of Sichuan province. Look for frozen favas with Hispanic foods or in the freezer section in your supermarket. If you want an even more substantial salad, just double the sauce and add cooked sweet potato glass noodles.

Active: 25 mins

Total: 25 mins

Servings: 4

Ingredients

- 1 cup frozen shelled fava beans, lima beans or edamame (5 ounces)
- 1 small clove garlic, minced
- 1 tablespoon water

- 2 tablespoons flakes/sediment from Sichuan chili oil (see Tips)
- 2 teaspoons Sichuan peppercorn oil (see Tips)
- 1 teaspoon toasted sesame oil
- 1 teaspoon reduced-sodium soy sauce
- 1 teaspoon Zhenjiang black vinegar (see Tips)
- 1 teaspoon honey
- 1 pinch Pinch of kosher salt plus 1/4 teaspoon, divided
- 3 large red radishes, julienned
- 4 cups pea or radish sprouts
- 1 scallion, thinly sliced

Directions

1. Cook beans according to package directions. Drain and rinse under cold water. Pat dry.

2. Meanwhile, mix garlic and water in a medium bowl. Let stand for 3 minutes. Add flakes/sediment from chili oil, peppercorn oil, sesame oil, soy sauce, vinegar, honey and a pinch of salt; mix well.

3. Toss radishes with the remaining 1/4 teaspoon salt and let stand for 3 minutes. S□ueeze most of the moisture out of the radishes, then add them to the dressing. Add sprouts, scallion and the beans; gently toss to coat.

Tips

Tips: Sichuan chili oil: A Sichuan spice blend is infused into the oil, which is mixed with chile pepper flakes (not fried). The oil can be strained and the flakes used separately.

Sichuan peppercorn oil: A fragrant finishing oil infused with essential oils extracted from the Sichuan peppercorn. It has a smoother taste than the whole spice yet enough zing to wake up the mouth.

Zhenjiang black vinegar: Sometimes labeled "Chinkiang," this delicately sour rice vinegar seasoned with sugar and salt is used in virtually all cold Sichuan noodle and vegetable sauces, and in other sweet and sour dishes.

Nutrition Facts

Serving Size: 3/4 Cup

Per Serving:

122 calories; protein 4.5g 9% DV; carbohydrates 16.1g 5% DV; dietary fiber 4g 16% DV; sugars 4.8g; fat 4.8g 7% DV; saturated fat 0.7g 4% DV; cholesterolmg; vitamin a iu 1844.4IU 37% DV; vitamin c 44mg 73% DV; folate 10.9mcg 3% DV; calcium 37.1mg 4% DV; iron 1.9mg 10% DV; magnesium 16.5mg 6% DV; potassium 209.5mg 6% DV; sodium 225.3mg 9% DV; added sugar 1g.

Umami Veggie Burgers

These hearty veggie burgers have a touch of grated red beet as a nod to beef. Pile on your favorite toppings or skip the bun and serve with a big salad.

Active: 40 mins

Total: 40 mins

Servings: 4

Ingredients

- ⅔ cup walnuts

- 1 (15 ounce) can no-salt-added chickpeas

- 1 ½ cups cooked ☐uinoa

- 3 tablespoons Umami Paste (see Associated Recipes)

- 3 tablespoons potato starch

- 2 tablespoons finely grated red beet

- ¾ teaspoon kosher salt

- ¼ teaspoon ground pepper

- 2 tablespoons canola oil

- 4 eaches soft whole-wheat hamburger buns, toasted

Directions

1. Pulse walnuts in a food processor until coarsely ground. Transfer to a bowl. Add 1 ½ teaspoons chickpea li☐uid (aquafaba) from the can to a food processor. Rinse the chickpeas and add 1 cup to the food processor (reserve the rest for another

use); pulse to a coarse mashed texture. Scrape into the bowl with the nuts and add ☐uinoa, umami paste, potato starch, beet, salt and pepper. Stir to combine well.

2. Shape the mixture into 4 patties, using about ¾ cup for each. Heat a large cast-iron or nonstick skillet over medium-high heat. Add oil; when it is shimmering, add the patties. Cook, flipping once or twice, until very browned and crisp, 5 to 8 minutes total. Transfer to a rack and let cool for 5 to 10 minutes. Serve the burgers on buns.

Associated Recipes

Umami Paste

Nutrition Facts

Serving Size: 1 Burger

Per Serving:

498 calories; protein 14.1g 28% DV; carbohydrates 60.8g 20% DV; dietary fiber 9.7g 39% DV; sugars 6.3g; fat 23.5g 36% DV; saturated fat 2.2g 11% DV; cholesterolmg; vitamin a iu 70.7IU 1% DV; vitamin c 2.8mg 5% DV; folate 67.3mcg 17% DV; calcium 112.4mg 11% DV; iron 3.6mg 20% DV; magnesium 133.6mg 48% DV; potassium 523mg 15% DV; sodium 787.1mg 32% DV.

Strawberry & Bean Sprout Salad with Spiced Potatoes

Active: 25 mins

Total: 25 mins

Servings: 4

Ingredients

- 3 eaches dried small red chiles, such as chile de arbol, stemmed
- 2 teaspoons coriander seeds
- 1 teaspoon cumin seeds
- 2 tablespoons canola oil
- 2 eaches medium yellow or russet potatoes, peeled and cut into 1-inch cubes
- ¾ teaspoon kosher salt, divided

- 1 (7 ounce) package mung bean sprouts

- 1 ½ cups medium strawberries, ☐uartered

- ¼ cup finely chopped fresh cilantro

- 2 tablespoons lime juice

- 1 medium head Butter lettuce for serving

Directions

1. Heat a large skillet over medium-high heat. Add chiles, coriander seeds and cumin seeds. Toast, shaking the pan frequently, until the chiles blacken and the seeds turn reddish brown, 1 to 2 minutes. Transfer to a small bowl.

2. Add oil to the pan and heat over medium-high heat until shimmering. Add potatoes

and ½ teaspoon salt; cook, stirring occasionally, until crispy and cooked through, 8 to 12 minutes. Transfer to a medium bowl.

3. Meanwhile, finely grind the chiles and spices in a clean spice grinder or with a mortar and pestle.

4. Add the ground spices to the potatoes along with sprouts, strawberries, cilantro, lime juice and the remaining 1/4 teaspoon salt. Scoop the salad onto lettuce leaves and serve at room temperature.

Tips

Equipment: Spice grinder or mortar and pestle

Nutrition Facts

Serving Size: 1 1/4 Cups

Per Serving:

167 calories; protein 3.9g 8% DV; carbohydrates 23g 7% DV; dietary fiber 3.9g 16% DV; sugars 5.4g; fat 7.6g 12% DV; saturated fat 0.6g 3% DV; cholesterolmg; vitamin a iu 1243.5IU 25% DV; vitamin c 45.7mg 76% DV; folate 62.6mcg 16% DV; calcium 33.8mg 3% DV; iron 1.4mg 8% DV; magnesium 26.2mg 9% DV; potassium 646.5mg 18% DV; sodium 366.8mg 15% DV.

Grilled Broccoli Wedges with Herb Vinaigrette

Lightly charring the broccoli then finishing over indirect heat allows the stems to get tender without becoming too burnt.

Active: 10 mins

Total: 30 mins

Servings: 4

Ingredients

- 2 stalk (blank)s small broccoli stalks, trimmed and ☐uartered
- 4 tablespoons extra-virgin olive oil, divided
- ½ teaspoon salt, divided

- 2 tablespoons red-wine vinegar

- 2 tablespoons chopped fresh basil

- 2 tablespoons chopped fresh chives

- ½ teaspoon Dijon mustard

- ¼ teaspoon ground pepper

Directions

1. Preheat one side of the grill to medium-high; leave the other half unheated.

2. Toss broccoli in a large bowl with 2 tablespoons oil and 1/4 teaspoon salt. Grill the broccoli, cut-side down, over the heat, turning once halfway through, until lightly charred, 10 to 15 minutes total. Move to the unheated side, close the lid and cook

until the stalks are tender, 10 to 15 minutes more.

3. Meanwhile, whisk vinegar, basil, chives, mustard and pepper with the remaining 2 tablespoons oil and 1/4 teaspoon salt in the bowl.

4. Toss the broccoli with the vinaigrette to coat.

Nutrition Facts

Serving Size: 1 Cup

Per Serving:

154 calories; protein 5g 10% DV; carbohydrates 14g 5% DV; dietary fiber 1g 4% DV; sugars 5g; fat 10g 15% DV; saturated fat 4g 20% DV;

cholesterol 19mg 6% DV; vitamin a iu 4388.4IU 88% DV; vitamin c 133.3mg 222% DV; folate 103.1mcg 26% DV; calcium 73mg 7% DV; iron 1.4mg 8% DV; magnesium 37.5mg 13% DV; potassium 219mg 6% DV; sodium 348mg 14% DV.

Spicy Tomato & Arugula Pasta

The simplicity of this healthy pasta recipe makes it good family fare. For a touch of heat, mild Anaheim chiles are augmented with crushed red pepper and garlic.

Active: 30 mins

Total: 1 hr

Servings: 8

Ingredients

- 3 medium red tomatoes, diced

- 2 medium yellow tomatoes, diced

- 1 teaspoon kosher salt

- 1 pound whole-wheat angel hair pasta or spaghettini

- 3 tablespoons extra-virgin olive oil

- 3 medium shallots, chopped

- 3 cloves garlic, chopped

- 1 (14 ounce) can crushed tomatoes

- 2 eaches Anaheim chiles, seeds and ribs removed, chopped

- ¼ cup chopped arugula

- 2 teaspoons chopped fresh oregano

- 1 teaspoon crushed red pepper

- ½ teaspoon ground pepper

- 8 pinches Grated Parmesan cheese for serving

Directions

1. Combine red and yellow tomatoes with salt in a large bowl. Let stand, stirring occasionally, until the tomatoes soften and release their juices, about 40 minutes.

2. Bring a large pot of water to a boil over high heat. Add pasta and cook according to package directions. Drain and rinse with cold water.

3. Dry the pot and add oil; heat over medium heat. Add shallots and garlic; cook, stirring occasionally, until the shallots soften, 3 to 4 minutes. Add crushed tomatoes and their juice; bring to a simmer. Cook for 5 minutes. Add the pasta, the fresh tomatoes, chiles, arugula, oregano, crushed red pepper and ground pepper. Cook, stirring, until hot, about 2 minutes. Serve topped with Parmesan, if desired.

Nutrition Facts

Serving Size: 1 ½ Cups

Per Serving:

305 calories; protein 9.4g 19% DV; carbohydrates 52.5g 17% DV; dietary fiber 7.3g 29% DV; sugars 6.4g; fat 7.3g 11% DV; saturated fat 0.8g 4% DV; cholesterolmg; vitamin a iu 774.5IU 16% DV; vitamin c 86mg 143% DV; folate 33.6mcg 8% DV; calcium 56.1mg 6% DV; iron 3.2mg 18% DV; magnesium 25mg 9% DV; potassium 657.9mg 18% DV; sodium 361.3mg 15% DV.

Roasted Purple Carrots with Black Sesame Dukkah

We love how the Egyptian nut, seed and spice blend dukkah adds aroma, flavor and texture to this otherwise simple purple carrot recipe.

Active: 15 mins

Total: 40 mins

Servings: 6

Ingredients

- 2 pounds purple carrots, halved or quartered lengthwise, if large
- 4 cloves garlic, peeled
- 3 sprigs fresh thyme
- 3 tablespoons extra-virgin olive oil, divided
- ¼ teaspoon salt plus 1/8 teaspoon, divided
- ¼ cup finely chopped unsalted pistachios
- 1 tablespoon black sesame seeds
- 1 teaspoon ground coriander
- 1 teaspoon ground cumin

Directions

1. Preheat oven to 400 degrees F. Line a baking sheet with parchment paper or foil.

2. Place carrots, garlic and thyme on the prepared pan. Drizzle with 2 tablespoons oil and season with 1/4 teaspoon salt; toss to coat. Roast until the carrots are tender but not browned, 25 to 30 minutes. Discard the thyme.

3. Meanwhile, to prepare dukkah: Heat a small skillet over low heat. Add pistachios, sesame seeds, coriander, cumin and the remaining 1/8 teaspoon salt; cook, stirring constantly, until warm and fragrant, 2 to 4 minutes. Remove from heat.

4. Arrange the carrots and garlic on a platter. Drizzle with the remaining 1 tablespoon oil and sprinkle with the dukkah. Serve warm.

Nutrition Facts

Serving Size: About 1 Cup

Per Serving:

160 calories; protein 2.8g 6% DV; carbohydrates 15.6g 5% DV; dietary fiber 4.8g 19% DV; sugars 6.8g; fat 10.4g 16% DV; saturated fat 1.4g 7% DV; cholesterolmg; vitamin a iu 22496.6IU 450% DV; vitamin c 8.7mg 15% DV; folate 29.5mcg 7% DV; calcium 59.3mg 6% DV; iron 0.9mg 5% DV; magnesium 26.9mg 10% DV; potassium 495.7mg 14% DV; sodium 239.9mg 10% DV.

Avocado and Egg Lunch

This Noom recipe from Platter Talk is fast and healthy!

Prep Time: 3 mins

Cook Time: 7 mins

Total Time: 10 mins

Course: lunch

Cuisine: American

Servings: 1

Calories: 398 kcal

Ingredients:

- 1 Avocado Peeled, sliced into 8 wedges
- 1 Egg poached

- 8 stalks Baby asparagus roasted

- 1 tbsp Balsamic vinegar

- Black pepper fresh ground

Directions

1. Pre-heat oven to 350° F. Place baby asparagus on small baking sheet, pour a little olive oil over it and shake and roll a bit, to help coat the stalks.

2. Pour a tablespoon of balsamic vinegar over the stalks and roll them in it.

3. Bring a small pot of water to a boil. Next place the asparagus in the oven, for 5 to 7 minutes, taking care to not leave it in too long! Poach the egg for about 3 minutes.

4. While the egg is poaching and asparagus is in the oven, peel and wedge the avocado and place on a plate in spiral form.

5. Place asparagus between wedges of avocado, and plate the poached egg in the center.

6. Garnish with fresh ground black pepper and additional balsamic vinegar if desired.

Keyword:

Avocado and egg, Avocado recipes, Egg and Avocado, Noom, Noom recipe

White Bean Chicken Soup

This slow cooker soup recipe is a meal the whole family will enjoy. Turn it into a rotisserie chicken recipe for added convenience!

Prep Time: 15 mins

Cook Time: 4 hrs

Total Time: 4 hrs 15 mins

Course: Soup

Cuisine: American, Mexican

Servings: 8

Calories: 218 kcal

Ingredients:

- 2 Roasted Chicken Breasts (shredded)

- 1 tbsp Olive Oil

- Salt and Pepper to taste

- 6 cups Chicken Broth reduced sodium

- 2 cups Salsa verde

- 2 tsp Cumin

- 32 oz Great Northern Beans Drained

Optional Garnishes

- Diced Cilantro Garnish

- Diced Green Onions Garnish

- Avocado Garnish

- Sour Cream Garnish

- Shredded Mexican Cheese Garnish

Directions:

1. Drizzle olive oil over chicken breast, salt and pepper to taste. Cook in a 350 degree oven for approximately 30-40 minutes or until cooked.

2. Let cool. Using 2 forks shred the chicken. Set aside.

3. In a crockpot, add chicken broth, salsa verde, cumin, white beans and shredded chicken. Cook on low for approximately 6 hours or on high for approximately 4 hours.

4. Serve as is or garnish with cilantro, green onions, avocado, sour cream or shredded Mexican cheese. Salt and pepper to taste.

Keyword

Healthy Chicken Recipe, Rotisserie chicken recipe, Slow Cooker Soup, White bean chicken soup

NOOM REVIEW (+ TROPICAL RASPBERRY SMOOTHIE)

This refreshing and delicious Tropical Raspberry Smoothie is healthy and easy to make!

Prep Time: 10 mins

Cook Time: 0 mins

Total Time: 10 minutes

Yield: 2 servings 1x

Ingredients:

- 1 cup water or milk of choice

- 1 cup frozen raspberries

- 1 banana

- 2 tablespoons lime juice

- 1 teaspoon coconut oil

- 1 teaspoon agave

- Ice

Directions

1) Blend all ingredients in a high-speed blender until smooth. Add ice, if desired.

Notes : Adjust sweetness to taste. You may need more or less sweetener depending on the tartness of the berries.

Nutrition:

Serving Size: 1 of 2 Calories: 200 Sugar: 32g Sodium: 2mg Fat: 2.7g Saturated Fat: 2g

Carbohydrates: 50g Fiber: 7.5g Protein: 1.6g

Cholesterol: 0mg

My Noom Green Meal A Big Bowl Of Yum

This meal is so flexible as you can eat it as a salad or as lettuce wrap sandwiches. FOODGASM! Since there's so much mystery behind NOOM, let me share just a glimpse of a meal. This recipe is an unofficially part of the Noom Green Foods list, so check out the list to verify. Inside the recipe, if you want to be a real rebel, you can spike it up with some fun Yellow and Red Food List items.

Prep Time: 10 minutes

Total Time: 10 minutes

Ingredients

- 14 oz can bean sprouts drained

- 2 Mini Cucumbers peeled and sliced

- ½ Organic Carrot, peeled, sliced.

- 3 Stalks of Celery, deveined and chopped.

- 1 Serving of Seeds of Change Organic Brown Basmati Rice Cooked

- Navel Orange peeled and divided into chunks

- Garlic Salt Dash

Optional Items (not green)

- 1 Tsp Soy Sauce

- 1 Tablespoon Feta Cheese

- 1 Tsp of Trader Joe's Champagne Dressing

Directions:

1. Make sure your shrimp are fully cooked, take off the tail, place in the bowl.

2. Next, add your bean sprouts (drained)

3. Now add the cooked brown basmati rice.

4. Then toss in fresh slices of peeled cucumber. Last, a peeled navel orange.

5. Rinsed and dried large buttercrunch lettuce leaves, plated. As said before, it's a big bowl of yum!

6. Optional items to add in as listed above: Feta, Vinaigrette, and soy sauce. Really add-ins are more a personal choice.

7. If you choose to dress this salad and you don't want any of the aforementioned,

consider lemon or lime freshly squeezed atop.

8. Dash with a bit of garlic salt if you like as well. Hold one buttercrunch leaf and then place any of the bowl contents into the lettuce leaf. Roll and enjoy it!

Notes: You can also use Belgian Endive instead of Buttercrunch, but it will scoop instead of wrap.

Nutrition Information: Yield: 1 Serving Size: 1

Amount Per Serving: Calories: 493 Total Fat: 17g Saturated Fat: 4g Trans Fat: 0g Unsaturated Fat: 12g Cholesterol: 16mg Sodium: 1005mg Carbohydrates: 74g Fiber: 7g Sugar: 18g Protein: 16g

Nutrition content varies based on veggies used by each person creating this meal.

Egg Breakfast Cups

featured in Recipes For A Healthy And Hearty Breakfast. Under 30 minutes

Ingredients:

for 6 servings:

- 5 eggs
- salt, to taste
- pepper, to taste

Mix and Match Fillings

- spinach, chopped
- tomato, diced

- onion, diced fine

- 1 bell pepper, diced fine

- 1 head broccoli, cut into small florets

- parmesan cheese

- cheddar cheese

Direction:

1. Preheat oven to 350°F (180°C).

2. In a measuring cup, beat the eggs until smooth. Set aside.

3. In a greased muffin tin, place your desired combination of fillings into each muffin cup.

4. Season each cup with salt and pepper.

5. Pour the beaten eggs into each muffin cup until the liquid almost reaches the top.

6. Bake for 20 minutes, until set. Enjoy!

Nutrition Information:

Calories 98 Fat 5g Carbs 5g Fiber 1g Sugar 2g Protein 7g

CONCLUSION

Noom is an app that you can access with a mobile device like a smartphone or tablet.

The app may help people lose weight by promoting low-calorie, nutrient-dense foods and encouraging healthy lifestyle changes.

If costs, accessibility, and a virtual style of health coaching don't sway your decision, Noom may be worth a try.